THE EUGÉNIE ROCHEROLLE SERIES

Intermediate Piano Duet

George Gershwin
Three Preludes — 1 Piano, 4 Hands

Arranged by Eugénie Rocherolle

T0079012

Cover photo courtesy of Photofest

ISBN 978-1-4768-8941-2

GERSHWIN® and GEORGE GERSHWIN® are registered trademarks of Gershwin Enterprises

Visit Hal Leonard Online at
www.halleonard.com

World headquarters, contact:
Hal Leonard
7777 West Bluemound Road
Milwaukee, WI 53213
Email: info@halleonard.com

In Europe, contact:
Hal Leonard Europe Limited
1 Red Place
London, W1K 6PL
Email: info@halleonardeurope.com

In Australia, contact:
Hal Leonard Australia Pty. Ltd.
4 Lentara Court
Cheltenham, Victoria, 3192 Australia
Email: info@halleonard.com.au

PRELUDE I

By GEORGE GERSHWIN
Arranged by Eugénie Rocherolle

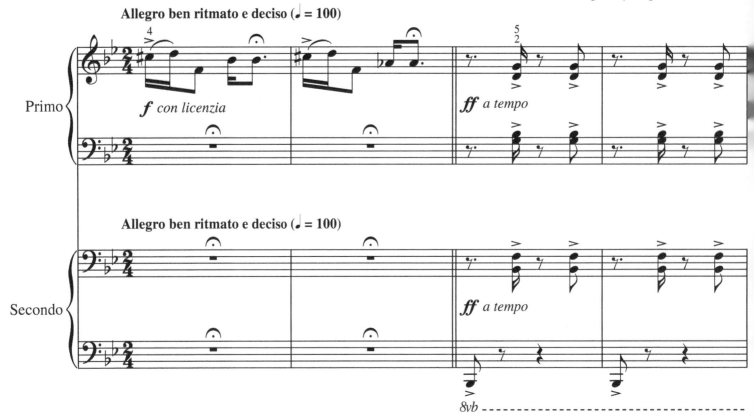

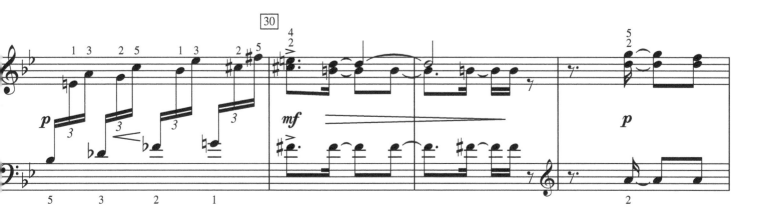

6

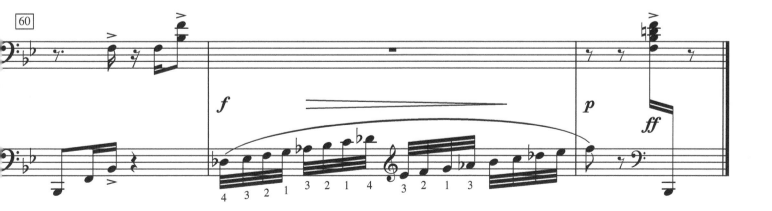

PRELUDE II

By GEORGE GERSHWIN
Arranged by Eugénie Rocherolle

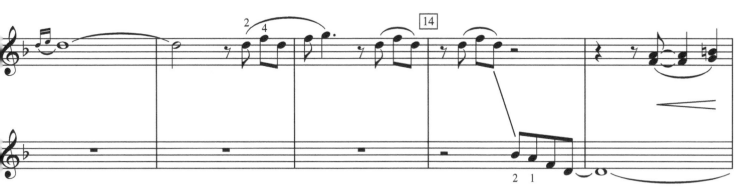

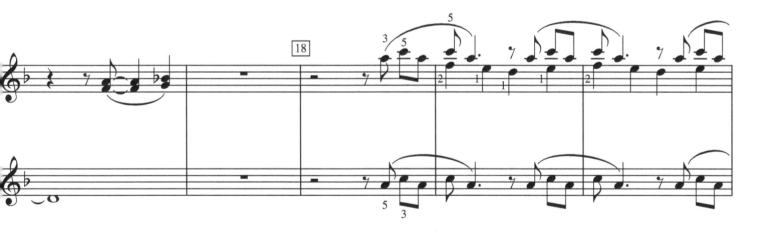

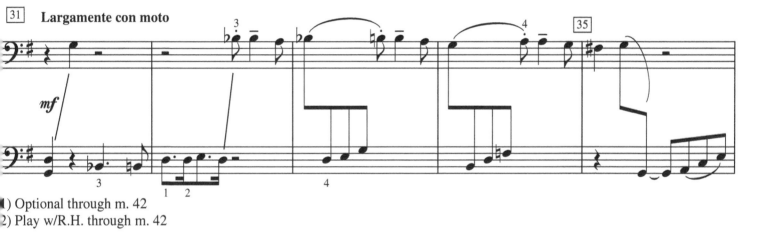

1) Optional through m. 42
2) Play w/R.H. through m. 42

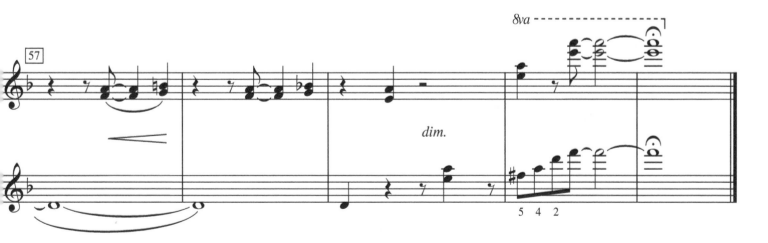

PRELUDE III

By GEORGE GERSHWIN
Arranged by Eugénie Rocherolle

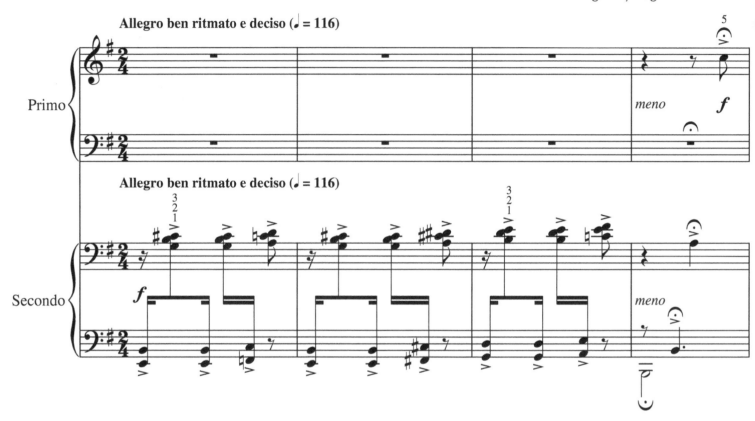

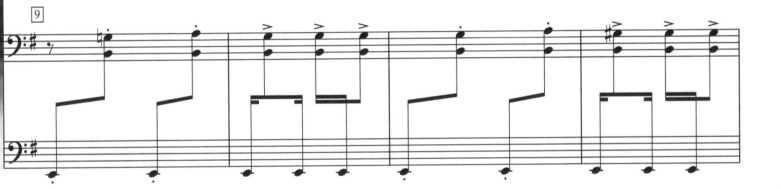

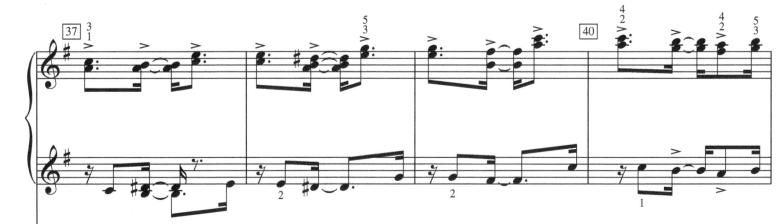

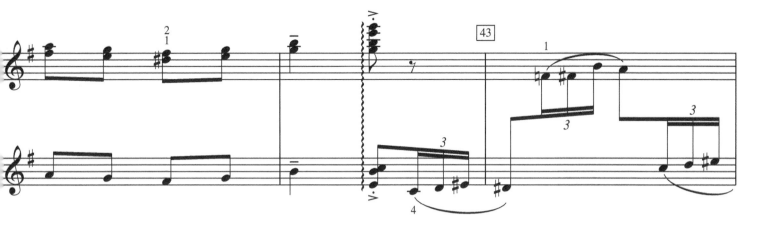

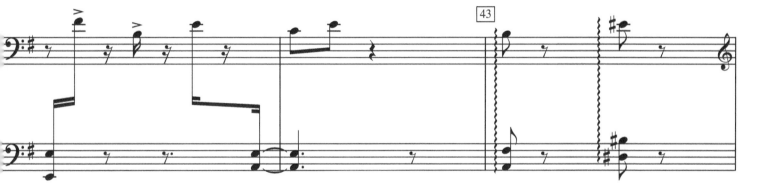

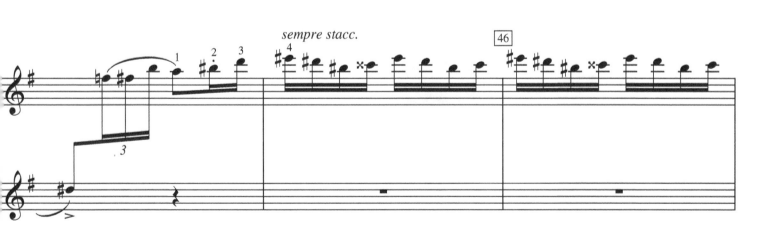

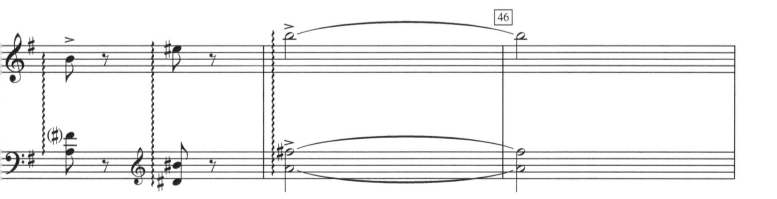

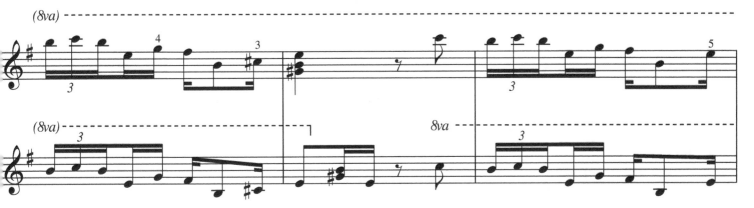

THE EUGÉNIE ROCHEROLLE SERIES

Offering both original compositions and popular arrangements, these stunning collections are ideal for intermediate-level pianists! Many include audio tracks performed by Ms. Rocherolle.

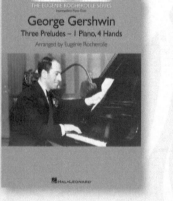
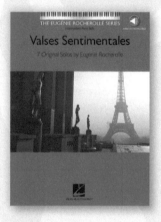

Candlelight Christmas
Eight traditional carols: Away in a Manger • Coventry Carol • Joseph Dearest, Joseph Mine • O Holy Night (duet) • O Little Town of Bethlehem • Silent Night • The Sleep of the Infant Jesus • What Child Is This?
00311808... $14.99

Christmas Together
Six piano duet arrangements: Blue Christmas • The Christmas Song (Chestnuts Roasting on an Open Fire) • Rudolph the Red-Nosed Reindeer • Santa Baby • Up on the Housetop • We Wish You a Merry Christmas.
00102838 .... $14.99

Classic Jazz Standards
Ten beloved tunes: Blue Skies • Georgia on My Mind • Isn't It Romantic? • Lazy River • The Nearness of You • On the Sunny Side of the Street • Stardust • Stormy Weather • and more.
00311424 .... $14.99

Continental Suite
Six original piano solos: Belgian Lace • In Old Vienna • La Piazza • Les Avenues De Paris • Oktoberfest • Rondo Capichio.
00312111 .... $14.99

Fantasia del Tango
Six original piano solos (and a bonus piano duet!): Bailando Conmigo • Debajo las Estrellas • Ojos de Coqueta • Promesa de Amor • Suenos de Ti • Suspiros • Tango Caprichoso.
00199978 ....$12.99

George Gershwin – Three Preludes
Accessible for intermediate-level pianists: Allegro ben ritmato e deciso • Andante con moto e poco rubato • Agitato.
00111939 .... $10.99

It's Me, O Lord
Nine traditional spirituals: Deep River • It's Me, O Lord • Nobody Knows De Trouble I See • Swing Low, Sweet Chariot • and more.
00311368 ....$12.99

Mancini Classics
Songs: Baby Elephant Walk • Charade • Days of Wine and Roses • Dear Heart • How Soon • Inspector Clouseau Theme • It Had Better Be Tonight • Moment to Moment • Moon River.
00118878 .... $14.99

Meaningful Moments
Eight memorable pieces: Adagio • Bridal March • Elegy • Recessional • Wedding March • Wedding Processional. Plus, arrangements of beloved favorites Amazing Grace and Ave Maria.
00279100 .... $9.99

New Orleans Sketches
Titles: Big Easy Blues • Bourbon Street Beat • Carnival Capers • Jivin' in Jackson Square • Masquerade! • Rex Parade.
00139675.. $14.99

On the Jazzy Side
Six original solos. Songs: High Five! • Jubilation! • Prime Time • Small Talk • Small Town Blues • Travelin' Light.
00311982 ....$12.99

Recuerdos Hispanicos
Seven original solos: Brisas Isleñas (Island Breezes) • Dia de Fiesta (Holiday) • Un Amor Quebrado (A Lost Love) • Resonancias de España (Echoes of Spain) • Niña Bonita (Pretty Girl) • Fantasia del Mambo (Mambo Fantasy) • Cuentos del Matador (Tales of the Matador).
00311369... $14.99

Rodgers & Hammerstein Selected Favorites
Eight favorites: Climb Ev'ry Mountain • Do-Re-Mi • If I Loved You • Oklahoma • Shall We Dance? • Some Enchanted Evening • There Is Nothin' like a Dame • You'll Never Walk Alone. Includes a CD of Eugénie performing each song.
00311928 .... $14.99

Romantic Stylings
Eight original piano solos: Cafe de Paris • Celebracion • Last Dance • Longings • Memento • Rapsodie • Reflections • Romance.
00300006 .... $9.99

Two's Company
Titles: Island Holiday • La Danza • Mood in Blue • Postcript • Whimsical Waltz.
00311883 ....$12.99

Valses Sentimentales
Seven original solos: Bal Masque (Masked Ball) • Jardin de Thé (Tea Garden) • Le Long du Boulevard (Along the Boulevard) • Marché aux Fleurs (Flower Market) • Nuit sans Etoiles (Night Without Stars) • Palais Royale (Royal Palace) • Promenade á Deux (Strolling Together).
00311497 .... $14.99

HAL•LEONARD®
www.halleonard.com

Prices, contents, and availability subject to change without notice and may vary outside the U.S.A.

0722